Craig Olson's
Decorating With Plants

To
Happy Reader

Cheers!

Craig Olson

Meadowbrook Press

18318 Minnetonka Boulevard • Deephaven, Minnesota 55391

Acknowledgements

Thanks to Holm and Olson Florists, Inc., St. Paul, MN, Thompson's Lighting Studio, Minnetonka, MN, and to the Dayton's Home Store, Edina, MN for their generous cooperation with preparations for this book. The Introduction is reprinted from "You Will Come to My Home Party," originally published in *The Grass Is Always Greener Over the Septic Tank*, by Erma Bombeck. Copyright © 1976. Used with permission of McGraw-Hill Book Company.

First printing March, 1981

Printed in the United States of America

Library of Congress Cataloging in Publication Data
Olson, Craig.
    Craig Olson's Decorating with plants.

    Includes index.
    1.   House plants in interior decoration.
I.   Title.   II.   Title: Decorating with plants.
SB419.045   747'.98   80-29579
ISBN 0-915658-31-3 (pbk.)

Cover Design and Art Direction: Terry Dugan
Interior Page Design: Marcia Conley
Illustrations: Janice St. Marie
Photography: Don Thoen
Managing Editor: Kathe Grooms

# Contents

In the last decade we've all come to expect houseplants to be a part of our lives, and they've moved into our homes, businesses and offices to stay. But no matter how much you like looking at your plants, you're missing a great deal of the fun they can give you if you don't let them actively enhance your life. If they're just sitting in the corner or hanging over there by the window, you're missing a bet!

That's why I wrote this book: to show you some of the many ways I've learned to make plants work for me. As a floral decorator and interior designer, I constantly make use of plants in my decorating and entertaining schemes. And in my televised and public appearances, I seem to mystify people when I take an English ivy, add a few things to its pot, put it in a novel container, and almost magically, create a centerpiece. But there's no magic to it — it's ridiculously simple! (As you're about to see.) Until you've really tried it, you'll never know how that English ivy of yours can be the center of attention — whether it's on the vanity in your bathroom, in a china pot in your French living room, or dressing up the table for an All-American dinner.

I also wrote this book to show you simple tricks and secrets for minimizing the work of caring for your plants, so I have included my favorite tips, along with a quick guide to the most popular plants. With these ideas for plant decorating and care, even if you're a novice you'll be assured of having happy, healthy plants that will really pep up your room and add a zing to your party as festive centerpieces. So read on, choose your favorite tips, give them a try, and experiment creatively on your own. I know you'll love it — and so will your plants!

Cristie Olsen

by Erma Bombeck

One Thursday night as I was preparing to go to a home hair-coloring party, I got a call from Dollie Sullivan.

"Guess what?" she said excitedly, "I am giving a plant party. Can you come?"

"What is a plant party?" I asked.

"It's where you bring your sick plants to be healed and to buy new ones. It's really different," she said and hung up.

I figured, why not?

The plant party attracted a group of people I had never seen before. I had been there only five minutes when someone wanted to go halvsies on a 100-pound bag of manure and a perfect stranger showed me her aphids.

"Girls! Girls!" said the plant representative, "I hate to break this up, but we've got a lot of ground to cover this evening. No pun intended. First, I want to introduce you to my friends." Gathered around her on little chairs were a half dozen or so potted plants. She began to introduce them one by one. "This is Florence Floribunda, Polly Pothus, Ginny Geranium, Irene Iris, Dorothy Daffodil, and Phyllis Potbound — we'll talk more about Phyllis later.

"Now, before we get to the sickies, I want each of you to answer roll call with your favorite insecticide.

"Very good," she said when we had finished. "Now you all have an opportunity to find out about how to deal with your sick plants, so if you'll bring them up one at a time, we'll talk about them."

The first was a woman who was near tears.

"What seems to be the problem?" asked the leader.

"They have icky boo boo on the leaves," she sobbed.

"You're not being too scientific, but I know what you mean," she smiled. "Can all of you see the icky boo boo in the back? In Latin, it's called *primus blosis*. Its common name is dust. When a leaf is covered with five or six years of dust, it can't breathe. It suffocates."

"What should I do?" asked the woman.

"Let's do something gutsy," she said. "Let's wash it." (The crowd cheered.)

Next up was a woman whose plant was in the final stages of deterioration. The leaves were ashen and crumpled limply to the floor. The leader studied it carefully. "Do you talk to your plant? Give it encouragement? The will to live? The incentive to grow?"

"I talked to it yesterday," she said, "but I didn't talk very nice to it. I called it something."

"What did you call it?" asked the plant lady.

The owner whispered the word in the leader's ear. She too turned ashen and crumpled limply to the floor.

Toward the end of the evening, we were given the opportunity to buy fresh, new plants to refurbish the ones in our homes. I chose a beautiful split-leaf philodendron with shiny, green leaves in a pot of mulch fluffed up at its feet like a pillow. That night as I paced the floor with the plant over my shoulder I patted it gently and thought, "What the heck. It beats burping Suckerware."

Part One

Creative Decorating Tips

Chapter 1

Plants to Suit Your Rooms

The first part of this book shows you how to have much more fun with your plants — and how to get them to work for you in your decorating and party schemes. Once you begin to think in terms of all the things that plants can do to blend with the function of your rooms, compliment your decor and add that sparkling touch to a gathering, you'll not be content to let your plants sit in the corner again. And they will love being the center of attention!

This chapter shows you how plants can best serve your decorating plans, room by room. It takes up different kinds of rooms — living rooms, kitchens, bathrooms — and discusses how best to compliment each room's look and function. You'll also find a list of plants that are especially well suited to each type of room. Read on and make your plans!

Living Rooms

The term living room is just what it says — a room where you live — so why not keep this room well-supplied with plants? No matter what direction the room faces, there are a lot of plants for you to choose from. The extra light from lamps that you turn on in the evening helps supplement the amount of light even a dark, north-facing living room offers plants. If your room does face north, a good idea, also, is to use light colors on the walls and in the carpet to get as much benefit from light sources as possible. The light thus won't be absorbed by dark surfaces.

If, on the other hand, your living room faces south, you won't have to worry as much about the amount of light. You will, however, have to make sure your plants are not placed right next to the glass so they won't burn.

Think how warm you got the last time you sat by an unshaded window. Well, a plant has a similar tendency to "cook." So be a little careful in placing plants near southern windows.

A living room with lots of plants can have such a cooling effect on hot summer days! Yet it can have an equally cozy effect on cold, gray winter days. Since this is where people spend time when they're at home, use a combination of plants — dark green, variegated and a few blooming ones — to make the room inviting.

Invite the plants listed below into your living room and have a party.

Dieffenbachia	**Pothos**
Dracaena	**Rubber Plant**
Marginata	**Schefflera**
English Ivy	**Splitleaf**
Grape Ivy	**Philodendron**

A pot of dark-green ivy and a jade-green schefflera combine well.

Dining Rooms

Today's dining room has gone through such an evolution that the room can be a part of the living room, the kitchen, or a separate area altogether. Whatever the situation is in your home, the dining area or room will seem more tranquil and appetizing, so to speak, with the addition of a few plants.

Imagine, if you will, a dining room without a chandelier. In its place, you may want to hang a selection of plants that you can keep trimmed to a certain length. For light, just insert a few candles into the soil and light them for an old-fashioned candle chandelier effect. Center one additional plant on the table itself with a few candles and you'll feel like you're serving dinner in a twinkling gazebo.

In a more formal atmosphere, put two beautiful flowing Boston ferns on pedestals, one on either side of a bay window or French doors leading to a terraced garden. Add two smaller ones in silver wine coolers set on the sideboard. Now you have a formal look with a touch of today.

Lovely wall brackets filled with plants can also liven up a dining room. Brackets can make a place for greenery in a room that doesn't always have much extra floor space. Again, repeat the same plants in a large tureen on the table; you'll carry out a theme of greenery! Also, this scheme always provides an instant centerpiece on the table.

The plants in the following list will all do well in a dining room.

Begonia	**English Ivy**
Boston Fern	**Geranium**
Coleus	**Grape Ivy**
Croton	**Peperomia**
Dieffenbachia	**Zebra Plant**

Swedish ivy and candles — instant chandelier, instant centerpiece.

Kitchens

Kitchens are marvelous places to grow plants for a variety of reasons. Let's face it: the dishes have to be washed eventually and the kids can go just so long without food, so you have to spend time in this room whether you want to or not. This gives you a good chance to keep a watchful eye on how the plants in this room are growing.

Besides, the water is right there. You don't have to carry a dripping watering can all through the house. Also, in most houses, a kitchen is a fairly bright room, so with a little luck your plants should grow well.

We all know what E.R.A. stands for (I can't think of a better room to put it into practice), but in the kitchen it could also stand for "Environmentally Relaxed Atmosphere." This atmosphere can be achieved by grouping your kitchen plants to get maximum benefit from them.

A miniature window greenhouse can replace the window over the sink for very little money. If this is not possible, two or three glass shelves can be attached to the window to provide space for massing those cuttings *so often* scattered all over the house.

Another place for plants is the eating area of the room. If there is space to have hanging plants instead of draperies, you can, with pots of sprengeri fern, transform this part of the room into a garden setting that will make the most boring breakfast become a real treat.

Don't forget the kitchen table. A six-inch pot of English ivy in a pretty basket, or an eight-inch clay saucer filled with an array of colorful cuttings, can provide you with an instant centerpiece. Other plants you could grow in this area are listed below.

Begonia   **Philodendron**
Coleus   **Sprengeri Fern**
English Ivy

Grouped mixed plants and a hanging pot of ivy relax this kitchen.

Hallways

We all dream of having the kind of house where, at the end of the hallway, there is a marvelous, cozy bay window seat that was obviously designed for curling up with a good book on a rainy day. If this is not the case with you (it isn't with me either, but I know this place has to exist *somewhere*), you can still create the same effect if you have a window. You can do this easily by placing a deacon's bench under the window and adding a few brightly colored pillows — and perhaps, if you're the favorite grandchild, throwing Grandmother's hand-crocheted afghan over the back of the bench. The next step, of course, is to add plants. Try a large Boston fern in a hanging basket (if the window faces east or north) or a splendid pot of sprengeri fern (for west or south exposures) — and you'll be all set for that book.

If, however, your hallway doesn't have any windows, you can still grow plants in it. Add some good track lighting to supplement the light that comes naturally from the rooms off the hallway. In this sort of situation, hanging pots of wandering Jew or Swedish ivy are two good choices. They can be hung near the artificial light. And there won't be anything on the floor to trip over when you raid the refrigerator at midnight.

All you need now is a couple of great pictures or some neatly framed posters to go along with your new green plants. Suddenly, this area of your house or apartment takes a whole new breath of life and is no longer just that dull passageway that connects one area to another.

Try a few of the following handy plants to create your own individual hallway atmosphere.

Boston Fern	**Sprengeri Fern**
Chinese Evergreen	**Swedish Ivy**
Grape Ivy	**Wandering Jew**
Pothos	

A Boston fern over a deacon's bench creates an inviting window seat.

Bedrooms

Most people don't spend too much time in their bedrooms, so the plants you put in them should be selected carefully. You simply won't pay as much attention to these plants because you're not around them as much, so they ought to be pretty hardy. But don't omit plants because you fear you'll neglect them. There is nothing that can make a bedroom more relaxing and create a private world better than plants.

Imagine a bedroom that's decorated with antique wicker furniture and a handmade patchwork comforter on the bed. Now add to this room a lovely tall palm in the corner and two piggyback plants clustered together on the dresser, all dressed up in wicker baskets. Who could ask for a "cozier" atmosphere than this?

Or what about a contemporary brass and wood four-poster bed sitting on an oriental rug, along with two French chairs and an antique armoire? A stately dracaena marginata in a lovely old jardinere placed in the corner will add drama because of its spinelike, irregularly shaped branches.

Another idea would be to attach a collection of antique wicker baskets and trays to the wall and do without a headboard. In a basket that has been well-secured to the wall, place a few lush Boston ferns to give a real South Seas feeling to your room.

Following is a list of plants that will add impact to any bedroom setting.

Areca Palm	**Piggyback Plant**
Boston Fern	**Pothos**
Cacti	**Schefflera**
Dieffenbachia	**Weeping Fig**
Dracaena Marginata	

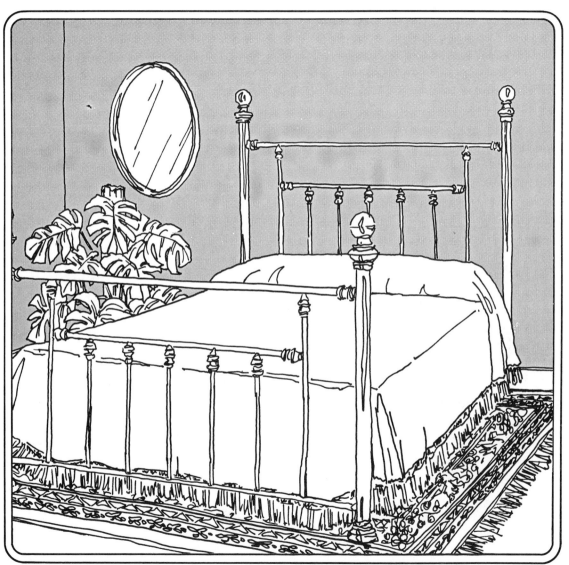

Carefree plants like split-leaf philodendrons are great for bedrooms.

Bathrooms

What better place is there to grow plants but in the bathroom? When you stop and think about it, a bathroom is the closest thing to a greenhouse in most homes. With the shower going and water being run many times during the day, this room is a vast source of humidity. No other room will give you this opportunity to grow plants.

Why not put three plants in clay pots, and then nestle these potted plants in the corner on the vanity? Next, put brightly colored guest towels rolled up in another clay pot sitting alongside the plants. Add a clay saucer brimming with guest soaps and use a large clay pot as a waste basket. On the corner of the tub, put a Boston fern planted in still another clay pot. On the walls, hang a trellis design wallpaper. You'll feel like the outside just came inside!

If your style is a bit more dressy, why not use brass pots for the plants and towels? A low brass ashtray can hold the soaps. Add a few antique brass candlesticks to reflect their glowing light in the mirror and heighten the drama. If you can install a pair of brass sconces and a brass chandelier, you'll be able to create an atmosphere where a relaxing soak in the tub will be truly elegant.

Unfortunately for those of us who live in apartments where the bathrooms have no windows, there is no plant grown that will survive. In this case, use a wallpaper with an abstract leaf design or an oversized leaf pattern to get the same effect.

Try a few of the following plants in your bathrooms for a pleasant atmosphere.

Dieffenbachia	**Palm**
English Ivy	**Pothos**
Ferns — all varieties	**Strawberry Begonia**
Grape Ivy	**Weeping Fig**
Miniature Schefflera	

Blooming begonias bring a splash of color to a bathroom.

Chapter 2

Plants to Fit Your Decor

Life styles are changing so rapidly these days — naturally, this change is being reflected in the ways people decorate their homes. Plants are being used to enhance all types of decor, as you'll see in this chapter. A roomful of great antiques will have a place (even a need) for green plants as well as will a very contemporary, modular atmosphere.

The important thing to remember is to purchase a plant that compliments your way of life and your style of furniture. Since every plant suggests a mood or style, make sure the ones you choose really do enhance the decor or scheme you develop. After each discussion of the popular decorating styles used these days, you'll find a list of plants that fit in well with these looks.

French

Although there are many variations possible, a true French room tends to be very soft with rounded lines and a delicate atmosphere. No two ways about it: a French room is going to look quite feminine.

This style of home decoration also tends toward the formal. When accented with china figurines and, perhaps, a collection of glass, French decor creates a restrained, fragile setting. Plants of the right type will enhance this feeling and will help pull the room together.

A home decorated in this style, whether with antiques or reproduc-

tions, would look best when accessorized by a lovely china pot brimming with English ivy and perhaps two Boston ferns on matching pedestals. Add to this a weeping fig in a stately brass pot that has been pruned into a ball shape, a reminder of the formal gardens in the Chateau country, and your room is complete.

The following plants will look very French for you.

Boston Fern	**Sprengeri Fern**
Ivy — all varieties	**Weeping Fig**
Tahitian Bridal Veil	**Whitmani Fern**

A pruned weeping fig brings topiary elegance to a restrained French study.

Traditional

Tranquil traditional is what I like to call it. Decorating with traditional furniture always gives a room such a secure look. It's that room where, when you walk in, you immediately feel at home. The tables are always mahogany; the wingback chairs are always Queen Anne; the fireplace (which is mandatory) is always lit. That's why the look is traditional — it's been pleasing people for years.

Lovely upholstered chairs with ottomans, a sofa upholstered in, perhaps, a quilted fabric, and gleaming mahogany tables are just so stable looking. The quieting effect of a traditional room does not call for a Bonzai tree or dracaena massangeana. Instead, pots of philodendron trailing from the fireplace, or full, lush philodendrons on a side table, look lovely in these rooms.

The other lovelies are listed below.

Arrowhead Plant   **Schefflera**
Dieffenbachia   **Splitleaf Philodendron**
English Ivy   **Zebra Plant**
Norfolk Island Pine

A blooming cyclomen, a lush fern and trailing ivy are traditional accents.

Contemporary

Contemporary styling is appearing nowadays in more and more homes, probably because it's so well suited to today's casual lifestyle. Such a style provides a perfect setting for our green friends. The softness of the foliage, along with the interesting angular effects some plants have, make a pleasing combination in home furnishings.

How about that room with chrome and glass coffee tables, modular wall units, and an arc lamp hovering over the conversation area? In a room like this, a spectacular dracaena marginata — or three Chinese evergreens clustered in the corner — would have a dramatic effect.

A room all decorated in white-upholstered furniture sitting on a parquet floor with an off-white area rug has a very subtle look. Add to this some green plants set into handsome baskets and — presto! The room is finished.

A combination of sleekly designed furniture covered in multi-colored plaids, stripes, and checks defines another contemporary look. What plant wouldn't feel at home in a room like this?

The following plants will look very good in a contemporary room.

Aralia Elegantissima	**Dracaena Warnecki**
Bamboo	**Peace Lily**
Chinese Evergreen	**Schefflera**
Dracaena Massangeana	**Weeping Fig**

Dramatic dracaenas and elegant peace lilies are thoroughly contemporary.

Country Casual

Who doesn't enjoy a country casual look? Quilted chintzes, tie-back draperies, lots of pillows, panelled walls, pewter lamps and a blazing fire all help set this comfortable and yet casual feeling. Colors are muted; patterns don't jump out at you. The furniture beckons and says, "Sit down and put your feet up!"

Let's add some plants now to complete the room. A Chinese evergreen in an antique basket would grow well and look good by a fireplace. These beauties require little light, so they are good in a panelled room. How about a pothos growing majestically on a pole to fill the corner that doesn't need a lamp or chair?

In a room like this, your plants will look well if all are placed into dark or antique baskets, since woven textures will look best with country casual furnishings. (Make sure you put in a liner.) However, if you're not an antique basket collector, an assortment of clay pots and saucers will look just as well.

The plants that will look best are as follows.

Boston Fern	**Peperomia**
Chinese Evergreen	**Piggyback Plant**
Croton	**Prayer Plant**
Grape Ivy	**Spider Plant**

Wood panels mean low light—Chinese evergreens on the hearth, pothos above.

Mediterranean

The heavy dark colors of wood and fabric associated with Mediterranean furniture dictate a look all its own. The furniture usually is not as refined as, say, Italian pieces are and has a more compact, "chunky" look.

Wood colors are usually dark stained oak; fabrics in darker greens, golds and reds are favorites. These materials are usually patterned so as to add even more weight to a room. In short, lots of carved wood, wall hangings, and wood and glass chandeliers say *Mediterranean.*

Furniture in this style goes well in a den where you want a warm, friendly feeling. A delicate Boston fern would look strange there, simply because it would be too delicate. Grape ivy would look better than English ivy for exactly the same reason: English ivy is more delicate in feeling. Collections of heavier, more substantial plants would charm this room: philodendron, schefflera and rubber plants, just to name a few.

The list below will help this decor even more.

Aloe	**Kangaroo Vine**
Fiddle-Leaf Fig	**Palm**
Jade Plant	**Snake Plant**

Chunky scheffleras and jade trees fit the woody Mediterranean look.

Victorian

Our ancestors really came up with a style that was all their own when they created the Victorian look. Softly curving sofa backs; marble-topped tables; swagging draperies; delicately turned table legs; beautiful fabrics of damask, brocade and velvet were and still are the characteristics of this style. Controlled clutter, with knickknacks everywhere, is part of that look too.

An aralia elegantissima would look like an uninvited guest in this setting. But a palm — a palm will look like it is holding court. And that's perfectly appropriate for a Victorian setting, isn't it?

Beautiful ceramic containers for the plants will also be a plus in this room. Don't use a basket here. Definitely not a basket!

Other plants that could hold court are the following.

Baby Tears	**Norfolk Island Pine**
Boston Fern	**Palm**
English Ivy	**Sprengeri Fern**

Palms and Victorian clutter go hand in hand—most properly, of course.

Williamsburg

Chamber music, powdered wigs, women in satin dresses and witty conversation all were part of the Williamsburg era. The refined, understated elegance of the era's furnishings also calls for refined plants.

Peace lilies placed in wine coolers on the sideboard would be elegant. A lovely fern set into a silver bowl that's on the hallway chest would be a real finishing touch. Weeping figs pruned into ball shapes, or at least trimmed so as not to be "wild" looking, would be pleasant additions too.

Because of the restrained elegance of furniture and fabric used in Williamsburg design, your plant arrangements should be restrained, *not* overdone. A lovely arrangement of dried flowers and dried baby's breath also are needed and welcomed additions to this room. Or a wreath made of the same dried flowers, perhaps with a few pheasant feathers as accents, can hang above the mantle.

The elegant, well-behaved plants listed below will compliment any Williamsburg room.

Baby Tears	**Swedish Ivy**
Boston Fern	**Weeping Fig**
Ivy	**Whitmani Fern**
Sprengeri Fern	

Williamsburg is refined, from peace lilies to ferns to furnishings.

Eclectic

Plants and eclectic decorating go so well together. But eclectic and "early attic" are not the same! "Early attic" can be fun for that first apartment. Grandma's wicker rocker and Mom's old sofa covered with a bright sheet, along with that wonderful trunk you found at the auction, welcome those hand-me-down cuttings stuck in jam jars.

Eclectic *could* be the same idea — only refined at least two hundred and ten times. The off-white straight-lined sofa, combined with two French chairs, a chrome and glass étagère, a Chippendale coffee table, two small contemporary benches covered in a flame-stitched fabric, all sitting on an Oriental rug, *is* eclectic.

A magnificent schefflera in a Chinese porcelain container will truly look beautiful in this setting. Now add a Boston fern (in the corner) hanging from an antique hook. A giant blooming peace lily in another corner will have its own impact. Fill in with other green plants and you will have a wonderful eclectic room.

Plants that mingle well are all those below.

Coleus	**Jade Plant**
Croton	**Norfolk Island Pine**
Diffenbachia	**Schefflera**
Dracaena Marginata	**You Name It!**

Floor plants like scheffleras mix and match well with hanging ferns.

❧❧❧❧ Chapter 3 ❧❧❧❧

Festive Plant Arrangements

I can't think of a plant that doesn't like to go to a birthday party (or any party, for that matter) to be admired and to enjoy the festivities. When you think about it, there's no reason why it should be ignored for special occasions.

That's the fun of plants. So many of them can be used as instant centerpieces and festive decorations that it boggles the mind. Let your imagination run wild — that's the point of this chapter. Don't be hesitant. Just go ahead and make that bow, add those candles and flowers, be a genius and hear the applause!

So think about all the plants you have around the house. Incorporate them with your own ideas and the ideas you're about to see and you will have great success as a decorator for any sort of gathering.

Basic Supplies & Tips

- **Scissors** — always handy for cutting ribbons and yellowed leaves.
- **Glass Tubes** — little vials to hold water for those flowers that magically make green plants bloom. Always fill tubes with water before you insert flowers in them, and *then* position them in the soil. You'll find a variety of sizes at your local florist's.
- **Florist's Foil** — much like kitchen foil, only it comes in pretty patterns and colors. It holds its shape once it's put around a pot; get it at the florist's by the yard or roll.
- **Ribbon** — All colors, widths and patterns are available. The best width for plant decorating is 1¼" wide. To make a bow, cut off about four yards of ribbon and form a figure-8 with the first two feet or so; twist the middle of the 8 and pinch it between your thumb and forefinger. With the next two feet, form another 8; twist and pinch it. Continue doing this until the bow is full enough for your taste. Then secure the center of the bow with another piece of ribbon if you're attaching it to a basket, or with wire if you're inserting it into some soil. If you're doing the latter, leave a "tail" of wire to stick into the soil. Note: precision won't pay off in bow-making! A sloppy bow will look great. Don't throw out used bows: carefully pin them to a hanger and store them in a closet until you want to use them again.
- **Wire** — use 24-gauge wire in 18" lengths, available at the florist's, for securing bows, silk flowers and other decorations to plants.
- **Candles** — 15" or 18" tapers work best for inserting into the soil. Change to fresh candles when they burn too close to the foliage; use the old ones in wall sconces or other candle holders.

Birthdays

Your child is going to be five this year. For the party, use colored construction paper for place mats. Attach colored balloons and crayons to wires and stick them into a piggyback plant. Add some extra paper and crayons to the table and the guests won't notice whether the cake is chocolate or marble!

If your best (and I mean your *best*) friend is having his or her fortieth birthday, try this centerpiece. Place a dead or dying plant in the middle of a broken basket. Just for dirty tricks, tie a black ribbon, possibly with something like "Sympathy" or "Unhappy 40th" pasted on it, to the basket. Then combine some dead flowers for a corsage. This will either end your friendship or make it stronger!

Piggyback with crayons and balloons

After Theater

Suppose you're at the theater and you spot some old friends you haven't seen in a long time. You decide to ask them over for wine and cheese after the play and to see your new house. On the way home, you try to think of something to spark up the coffee table which will help spark up the conversation as well. While your spouse takes your guests' coats, excuse yourself and run upstairs to the guest bedroom and bring down that orchid plant that just started to bloom. Put it in the middle of the table and you instantly have a posh centerpiece. Next, add some cheese served on a silver trivet, crackers in a silver basket, a few candles — you have the makings of a successful party, all centered around that spectacular orchid.

Blooming mocassin orchid

45

Formal Wine & Cheese

For a formal gathering, serve the wine in antique cut wine glasses. (This occasion calls for a fine smooth cheese and, perhaps, even homemade crackers.) If you're doing this in the very early spring, why not add to this party some delicate paperwhite narcissus in a beautiful Chinese bowl? Place candles in multi-height silver candlesticks. Voila! You have an elegant centerpiece that will last way past the party. Stir into this some chamber music on the stereo, and your party could be billed as the occasion of the year.

Paperwhite narcissus

Informal Wine & Cheese

Wine and cheese don't always need to be so elegant. The same ingredients, arranged in a different way, can be equally casual. Grow your paperwhite narcissus in four-inch clay pots that can be clustered on a large clay saucer, placed on a bare wood table. Just before the party, fill in the saucer with fresh, crisp parsley and these pots of plants will look like they're in a lovely little green haven. Serve the wine in simple crystal glasses and both the cheese and crackers on clay saucers. See the difference?

Paperwhite narcissus with parsley

46

Peanuts & Beer

Peanuts and beer can be served a number of different ways. Granted, wearing a T-shirt, sitting in front of the T.V. and drinking the beer out of a can is one way. But it's not the only way. The beer can be served in chilled pewter mugs, with lots of salted almonds and peanuts mounded in pewter bowls. Everything here should surround a great grape ivy plant, studded with eighteen-inch tiny tapers and placed in the middle of the coffee table. The final touch is to light the fire and candles before inviting everyone to sit on pillows around the coffee table.

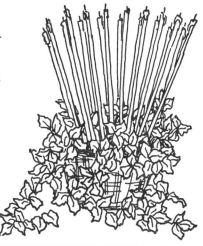

Grape ivy and tapers

Champagne & Caviar

Let's make this party a real smash! First, mortgage the house for the extra cash you'll need to pay for the three waiters who'll serve the champagne. Naturally, the plants to make this party must be nothing but the most regal, elegant, etc., etc., etc. of all plants — in this case, blooming white Cattleya orchids. If need be, go out and rent eight or ten of these beauties. Placing them here and there near candles will create the sense of opulence that you're after. Serve with cut crystal and sterling. Why not make this cocktail party black tie, and be the talk of the neighborhood?

Cattleya orchids

Brunches

Planning brunch menus is easy, and so is creating their centerpieces. Some ideas: get a lovely yellow mum and two loaves of French bread. Place the mum at one end of an antique wooden box. Tear, and I mean *tear*, the loaves in half and place them, ragged side up, in the other half of the box (if there's space left over, tuck in a small pot of English ivy). You're all set!

For a totally different look, place a pot of English ivy in a china or pottery bowl just slightly wider than the pot. Now take some crisped-up leaf lettuce and gently nestle the leaves around the plant (to act as a liner). Next, take other lettuce leaves and cut the bottom half off each one. Nestle the pretty tops in and around the ivy. If you want to get even more festive, place seven daisies in tubes of water and insert them into the ivy's soil. Imagine this crisp centerpiece on a spring green tablecloth, with white napkins and green and white dishes ... what a cool, refreshing effect.

If formality is what you're after, it's also easy to achieve by placing blooming African violets in individual silver Revere bowls and lining them down the table. For an even more formal look, just snip a blossom from each plant and tuck one into each napkin. Place the bowls on a pale pink cloth, use some antique Limoge serving plates and crystal wine glasses — suddenly, the whole table is in beautiful, elegant harmony.

Mums, bread and ivy

African violets, blossoms on napkins

All-American Dinners

Roast beef, mashed potatoes, corn on the cob, and good old Mom's apple pie are as American as you can get. Now let's do the table. An English ivy with red carnations in glass tubes in the soil will look great. Sprinkle some small American flags among them and add a blue table cloth, white dishes and white napkins tied with red, white and blue ribbon. Your table will be so patriotic, don't be surprised if George or Betsy shows up. Here's another all-American favorite: hamburgers and french fries served in a basket lined with a red and white gingham napkin. They'll also look great on the same table.

English ivy, red carnations, flags

Candlelight Dinners

Candles, candles, candles and more candles can transform any room. To do this, hang three wandering Jew baskets at different heights in each of two corners of the dining room. Put another one in a crystal compote on the table. Firmly, but gently, insert into each plant three eighteen-inch white candles, light them, and voila! — your T.V. dinner tastes like a gourmet delight. Delicious — more, more.

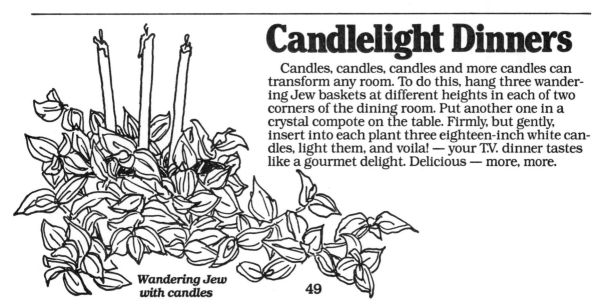

Wandering Jew with candles

49

Italian Dinners

Take an eight-inch pot of Swedish ivy (camouflaged just for tonight as Italian vine) and insert ten to twelve tiny taper candles into its soil. Put it in a pretty wicker basket garnished with a red, white and green striped bow. Place the plant on a red and white checked table cloth. Add people, wine and lasagna and you're ready for a festive Sunday night supper.

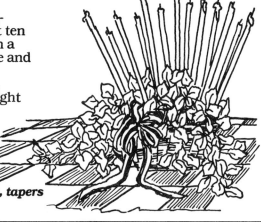

Swedish ivy, tapers and a bow

Salad Dinners

Diets, diets ... who's not on a diet these days? For those calorie-counting dinners, let's serve beautiful, tangy, crisp salads. For the salad dinner, try a salad centerpiece. French tinware baskets brimming with chive and parsley plants would be perfect. Line the baskets with moss for a refreshing woodsy effect. Serve the salads in crystal bowls on French tinware plates and no one will care that there's no chocolate mousse for dessert.

Blooming chive and parsley in tinware

Game Dinners

A wild game dinner definitely calls for a game plan. Will it be pheasant under glass or on a clay saucer? If the clay saucer look is what you want, here's how to do it. On the table, cluster some old wooden candleholders. Next, fill some small wooden boxes with tiny ferns. Because this will probably be in the fall, add a few gourds. Oh! the clay saucers. Use ten-inch ones lined with clear plastic saucers as the dinner plates. Sounds a little like you're roughing it tonight, but it will be a wonderful meal.

Tiny ferns in wooden boxes

Baby tears, coleus, geranium

Potluck Dinners

What's more fun than potluck? Call the neighbors in the afternoon and invite them for potluck supper. With the variety of food you'll have, here's the time for using some variety in a centerpiece. Cluster three or four different plants — a baby tears, a small coleus, a blooming geranium, and a strawberry begonia — on the table. Mix in a few votive holders with candles along with tapers in assorted candlesticks. Use a plain cloth with different colored napkins. Potluck dinner, potluck centerpiece, potluck table — have fun!

Spring Buffets

Boston ferns and pussy willows are wonderful together for a spring buffet. Take a chunky Boston fern and place it in a beautiful yellow pot. Next, add some pussy willows — about two dozen of them. They will look like they are growing straight out of the fern when placed near the center of the plant. Wire a few fake yellow canaries to the pussy willows. Now the fun touch. In the fern, hide a battery-operated bird chirper and your guests will almost believe the canaries are real!

Ferns and pussy willows

Fall Buffets

If spring came and went and you didn't have that buffet, try this idea in the fall. Take the same Boston fern, but now add some dried brown eucalyptus leaves to it. Hide the pot with some natural-colored burlap. The brown and green together make such a lovely combination. Set dark woven runners, earth-toned pottery dishes and dark green heavy glasses on the table. What could be a warmer look? Light the fire and your buffet will be a success.

Ferns and eucalyptus

Formal Picnics

Elegant ain't bad for a picnic. Round card tables set out on the lawn with flower-printed cloths can be sensational. Buy sheets during the white sales to cut them into cloths that will hang all the way to the ground. What a pretty effect they'll have, set against the green of the grass. A six-inch wicker basket with a pot brimming with parsley set into it will complete each table.

Parsley in a wicker basket

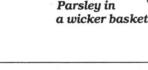

Informal Picnics

Red and white checked tablecloths seem to have been invented just for picnics. Four-inch clay pots, brimming with geranium plants and lined up and down the picnic table, will be sensational. Eight-inch clay saucers (preferably new ones) can easily hold a hamburger and potato salad along with chips and pickles. Ten-inch clay pots can be the serving dishes for the tossed salad as well as the potato salad and chips. Just make sure they've been washed well before using.

Geraniums in clay pots

Patio Picnics

Here's a special tip for the umbrella table. Use a gelatin mold to make your centerpiece. Punch holes in the bottom of the mold for drainage. Plant it with moss roses, or pansies, or any garden plant that will stay short and flower all summer. Place the mold in the middle of the table. Now, put the umbrella stem right down through the mold and through the table. What's easier than that! A centerpiece that will last all summer and fit around the pole of the umbrella — brilliant!

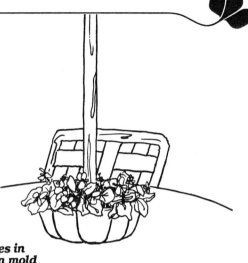

Pansies in gelatin mold

Hot-Weather Picnics

White begonias in clay pots painted white can look so cool. You might want to try this look in August when the temperature soars on your picnic day. Blend in some white plates (pottery or paper), yellow and white printed paper napkins, and the atmosphere will be *cool.* These white begonias are a blessing in disguise. Use them with any colored cloth — lime green, pink, yellow, sky blue — and see how your table changes.

Geraniums in clay pots

Wedding Flowers

English ivy, with its delicate foliage, is so much a part of a wedding. There's hardly a bridal bouquet that doesn't have a sprig or two of ivy in it. I even made an ivy skull cap for the mother of the bride once. She took the hat apart after the wedding, rooted the sprigs, and started new plants. On her daughter's first anniversary, she presented her with a lush pot of ivy as a remembrance of the wedding.

For centerpieces, place English ivy plants in white baskets. Add white roses in tubes of water, or — for a less formal look — yellow and white daisies. This can be so pretty and fresh-looking, and you can rent the plants and buy the flowers inexpensively from a florist.

English ivy with daisies

Wedding Gifts

You're invited to a wedding. "Oh, how nice," you think at first, and then, "what will I give them for a present?" Here's a thoughtful, exciting, *simple* idea: send them a plant a month. Just ask a florist to deliver a seasonal flowering plant on the first of each month. (This is a super idea for birthdays and anniversaries, too.) Or else send a lush green schefflera or a dramatic dracaena to the couple's new house or apartment after they return from their honeymoon. If you know they have plants already, you might want to send a nest of baskets of various sizes, but all the same design. Into one of the baskets, set a new plant. This way, the couple will have both a new plant and coordinated baskets for the older ones.

Nesting baskets with a new plant

Housewarming Gifts

Color and confusion can go hand in hand. Think about this when you know some friends are moving into a new house. Have a colorful mum, or cineraria, or azalea plant sent to their new house on moving day. The dash of color will be a sign that you care and also will make the move much more pleasant.

Plants of any kind are a welcome present at any housewarming party. Imagine a young couple with their first house. They probably don't have enough furniture to fill it up. A large plant in a bare corner will help their room look a lot more finished and less empty.

Moving from a first house to a larger house means even more corners to fill. A floor plant for a corner, a dish garden for a table or shelf, a hanging basket for the porch, even a pot of geraniums for the front stoop — all say the same thing: "Love, and Happy New House." Nothing is easier or nicer.

People choosing the condominium way of life would love a plant, too. One word of caution though: don't go overboard on the size of the plant. Many condominiums are scaled down in size, so scale down your green gift as well. A pretty plant for a coffee table will be better than a large schefflera for the corner.

Snake plant, jade tree and ivy

Get Well Gifts

Bulb plants are wonderful gifts for people who are going to be confined to bed for a while. There's something so cheery about watching a bulb plant grow. Amaryllis in the fall and winter is a real treat. Paperwhite narcissus bulbs are another pleasure for autumn invalids. They go from planting to blooming in about six weeks. Springtime patients enjoy watching a hyacinth or tulip or crocus come into bloom and older friends in nursing homes also enjoy seeing these, along with our smiling faces. Don't forget them.

For a good friend with a good sense of humor, buy a bedpan — yes, that's right. Take it to a greenhouse and have it planted with assorted green plants (or even cacti). It's guaranteed to get a rise out of your favorite patient.

Otherwise, try a yellow mum in a yellow wicker basket with a perky bow, or an African violet planted in a terrarium with a little moss and some miniature ferns. Or a small brass box planted with ivy and a cymbidium orchid in a tube of water. For color and cheerfulness, try any type of hanging plant in a bright basket with ribbon streaming from the hanger. Nothing is more festive.

***Pothos in hanging
basket with bow***

❦Holidays

Holidays can be so much fun. Let your imagination run a little wild and decorate away. For Valentine's day, take your miniature ferns, stick several scarlet baby roses in each, and group them in a plain white china bowl. Put some moss around the bases of the ferns, turn the lights down and the music up, and you're set for a romantic evening!

Take a yellow bushel basket and add some colored Easter grass around the edge. Place a lily plant in the midst of all this. Now scatter some jelly beans over the top of the grass and add a plaid bow. It's an informality the lily didn't know it had. For another Easter trick, place a number of spring blooming plants into a large round basket. Next, add a few pots of ivy dripping over the edge, pussy willows for height, and, again, the Easter grass for fill and color. How fresh and inviting!

Scoop a pumpkin out, settle a pot of grape ivy into it, place some orange candles in the ivy, add a black bow, and you're all set for Halloween.

A basket filled with a bronze mum plant, some Indian corn, gourds and wheat will dress up any Thanksgiving table.

Red poinsettias. Try this for a change. Trim with green and white checked florist foil. Add a red and white polka dotted bow. Suddenly, that poinsettia can look pretty perky. Or, what about adding one to a long, low basket? Mix in some evergreen branches and a few pine cones, and holiday magic is yours.

*Easter lily
with grass
and jelly beans*

*Poinsettia and bow
in florist's foil*

*Pumpkin with grape ivy,
candles and bow*

Friendship Gifts

What would we do without our friends? And what could be a nicer way to be a friend than giving someone a plant? A flowering plant can be so appreciated by someone who has had a death in the family or is merely feeling down in the dumps.

Or how about a friend who is taking a cruise? Your hometown florist can wire another florist in the port city to order a flowering plant and have it delivered to the stateroom.

What nursery would be complete without a plant? Send the new mother and baby a dish garden. Add to this a few cut flowers in tubes of water. Colorful for the hospital, green for the nursery.

**Dish garden
with cut flowers**

You-Name-It Arrangements

Virtually *any* lush plant you have can become a centerpiece with the addition of a few silk flowers, some candles and a gorgeous bow. On the cover of this book you see a Boston fern, all decked out. Vary the color composition and you can make a red-and-green Christmas (or Valentine's) arrangement, a yellow-and-green spring arrangement, a pink-and-green birthday (or Mother's Day) arrangement — to give you just a few combinations. Consider the occasion, your table or buffet setting, and your decor; then look around, pick out a healthy plant, and go to town!

**Fern, candles,
silk flowers and
bow**

Part Two

Plant Care Tips

Chapter 4

Choosing the Right Plant

The second part of this book will help you to have the most healthy, attractive plants possible with the least possible chance for disappointments. Whether you're a novice or an old hand (or thumb) with plants, I think you'll find lots of new tips and helpful ideas here.

When you come right down to it, perhaps the biggest secret in putting together a houseful of beautiful, thriving plants is to know what plants do best where, or what plants to avoid if you're not so hot at growing things in the first place. This brief chapter gives you lists of easy-to-grow, hard-to-grow, and other sorts of plants so you can choose the right plant for your needs. The lists are by no means exhaustive, but they will give you a starting place for a collection that will be fun to care for and great for your decorating plans.

Choosing the Right Plant

Ease of Care

EASIEST	HARDEST

EASIEST

Fortunately, there are some plants that are so easy to grow that caring for them is like rolling off a log. When people first start out growing plants, it is much better for their egos to start with the easy ones and work towards the hard ones. We all feel guilty about something in our lives, so at this point, let's not add dead or dying plants to our burdens!

As for what varieties to start out with, the following list will help get you started towards turning that thumb of yours green. Some of them are floor plants, some are perfect for that great antique trunk you're using for a coffee table and others are happy anywhere.

☐ **Cacti**
☐ **Corn Plant**
☐ **Dieffenbachia**
☐ **Dracaena Marginata**
☐ **Grape Ivy**
☐ **Peace Lily**
☐ **Peperomia**
☐ **Ponytail Palm**
☐ **Pothos**
☐ **Schefflera**
☐ **Splitleaf Philodendron**

HARDEST

There are certain plants that were developed only for the purpose of testing people's patience. Just when you think you really have a green thumb and can grow anything, you buy one of these very difficult plants. Leaves fall off or turn yellow, the plant wilts, and all your confidence goes flying right out the window. Take heart! The best of us have had bad luck at times with our plants.

When this happens, my only advice to you is to grin and bear it, and whatever else happens, *don't* buy that variety of plant again. It's just not worth it — financially or emotionally. Stay away from the ones listed below unless you have ideal conditions, a strong ego, lots of patience — and luck.

☐ **Balfour Aralia**
☐ **Gardenia**
☐ **Hibiscus**
☐ **Maidenhair Fern**
☐ **Ming Aralia**
☐ **Orange Tree**
☐ **Tahitian Bridal Veil**
☐ **Whitmani Fern**

LOW LIGHT

When I think about growing plants, the first thing that comes to mind is "Let there be light!" People naturally assume that plants want to sit in front of a window all day. Granted, there are a lot of plants that do require the feeling that they are in Miami, but, thank heavens, there are some that would prefer to stay out of the light and not soak up all those "rays."

Imagine the room that faces north and gets no direct sun at all. On top of that, the room happens to be the family room that is panelled with dark wood. What, oh what will grow? Fortunately, there are some plants that will find this room a haven. Read on and acquaint yourself with the following plants that are just a little "abnormal."

- ☐ **Begonia**
- ☐ **Chinese Evergreen**
- ☐ **Corn Plant**
- ☐ **Dracaena Marginata**
- ☐ **Grape Ivy**
- ☐ **Palm**
- ☐ **Peace Lily**
- ☐ **Philodendron**
- ☐ **Snake Plant**
- ☐ **Wandering Jew**

BRIGHT LIGHT

Unlike those low-light plants, for others, the brighter the light, the better. There are many plants that are just not happy unless they are being sun-drenched in a south or west exposure.

This a good thing too, since so many contemporary homes have walls of glass for those life-giving rays to come flowing through. The plants that love the sun will flourish unbelievably in such environments, and you'll see a ficus benjamina or schefflera send out leaf after leaf in them. Talk about sun-worshippers — they are fanatics. It's almost as if they know how fashionable a tan is. The list of the most common of these is below.

- ☐ **Aloe**
- ☐ **Cacti**
- ☐ **Coleus**
- ☐ **Geranium**
- ☐ **Hibiscus**
- ☐ **Jade Plant**
- ☐ **Kalanchoe**
- ☐ **Orange Tree**
- ☐ **Peperomia**
- ☐ **Schefflera**
- ☐ **Weeping Fig**

Space Needs

SMALL SPACES	LARGE SPACES

Happily for us all, there are small plants that stay small. The corner of the desk can't take a big, sprawly vine. A little end or side table doesn't care for a great big plant. The kitchen window sill won't be bothered with giants. Neither will the corner of the vanity in the bathroom or that narrow wall shelf in the hall.

There are many green plants that, although not miniatures, never grow to be regal floor plants or hanging plants six feet long. Small plants, all in the same type of pot, look very pretty clustered on a coffee table or lined up on the kitchen window sill. A few of the small plants available are listed below.

- ☐ **African Violets**
- ☐ **Aloe**
- ☐ **Baby Tears**
- ☐ **Boxwood**
- ☐ **Cactus**
- ☐ **Echevaria**
- ☐ **Kalanchoe**
- ☐ **Oxalis**
- ☐ **Pandanus**
- ☐ **Peperomia**

It's so refreshing to walk through a store or office building and be surrounded by lush, green foliage. The plants are not only important to today's decor, but make a very relaxing atmosphere in which to conduct business.

Many of the plants that are available today will grow into small trees when given the proper care. The larger the pot, the greater the area for roots to develop and support more growth. The excellent light available in ultra-modern buildings also encourages their growth.

Many of these plants will also do well in areas of homes that need spaces filled with green. (If it's the right size when you get it, keep a plant a little root-bound to prevent its getting out of hand.) Those listed below will soon be too large for the coffee table.

- ☐ **Aralia Elegantissima**
- ☐ **Dracaena Marginata**
- ☐ **Ming Aralia**
- ☐ **Norfolk Island Pine**
- ☐ **Palm**
- ☐ **Rubber Plant**
- ☐ **Schefflera**
- ☐ **Splitleaf Philodendron**
- ☐ **Weeping Fig**

Special Places

INDOOR-OUTDOOR

Spring and fall are when you have to worry about putting plants outside or bringing them in. Unless, of course, you live in sunny California.

In northern climates, it is better to wait until after May 15th to set plants out. Jack Frost still can be at work before that — believe me, I know. Next, you'll want to make sure that the sunlight is not too hot and direct. Plants being brought out from a shady area of the house won't be able to take the hot outdoor sun.

In the fall, make sure you clean your plants, check them for bugs, and use an insecticide spray to ensure that you're not bringing any pests into the house. The following plants will flourish indoors or out.

- ☐ **Begonia**
- ☐ **English Ivy**
- ☐ **Geranium**
- ☐ **Grape Ivy**
- ☐ **Hibiscus**
- ☐ **Impatiens**
- ☐ **Jade Plant**
- ☐ **Schefflera**
- ☐ **Sprengeri Fern**
- ☐ **Weeping Fig**

OFFICES

The last time you went to see your doctor, lawyer, dentist, etc., what did you see? Right! Diplomas and plants all over the place. Hanging plants, floor plants, desk planters and whatever. Perhaps you work in an office filled with plants as well. If so, there are two things to remember. Have only one person in charge of the watering can. We all know what happens when everybody thinks the other guy did it.

The other thing to remember is to buy plant saucers on wheels for those plants that are in offices with no windows. That way, the last thing Friday afternoon, you can wheel the plants out to a spot where there is natural daylight and leave them there until Monday morning. Check the following plants when you furnish your office.

- ☐ **Chinese Evergreen**
- ☐ **Dracaena Marginata**
- ☐ **Grape Ivy**
- ☐ **Palm**
- ☐ **Peace Lily**
- ☐ **Philodendron**
- ☐ **Pothos**
- ☐ **Rubber Plant**
- ☐ **Schefflera**
- ☐ **Wandering Jew**

Special Plants

MOST COLORFUL

Whenever people talk or think about indoor plants, they always think green. That's probably because there is the "green thumb" theory; plants are grown in *green*houses; and you have to dish out some green stuff to buy them. But wait a minute! There are all types of plants that are very colorful. These plants can make the dullest room come alive. I'm not suggesting that your room is dull because you don't have a colorful plant, but one might help. The list below gives you names of plants to grow that will brighten any corner.

- ☐ **Caladium**
- ☐ **Chinese Evergreen**
- ☐ **Croton**
- ☐ **Dieffenbachia**
- ☐ **Pothos**
- ☐ **Snake Plant**
- ☐ **Variegated Ivy**
- ☐ **Variegated Peperomia**
- ☐ **African Violets**
- ☐ **Wandering Jew**

WATER-LOVING

Believe it or not, there are some plants that thrive with too much water. Not only will they tolerate constantly wet soil but they'll also live in water with all the soil washed off their roots. If you love to over-water and then water plants again, you will simply adore a collection of these plants.

Grow some in colored glass bottles and vases in a window with glass shelves. Just take your plants, wash all the soil off and make sure the roots are nice and clean. Then arrange the plants in the vases for a stunning, sparkling, living stained glass window effect. Be sure to change the water periodically. Also, the plants will grow best if they have filtered, rather than direct, sunlight. Direct sun has a tendency to burn them.

The plants below will grow for at least a year in vases of water.

- ☐ **Chinese Evergreen**
- ☐ **Coleus**
- ☐ **Grape Ivy**
- ☐ **Pothos**
- ☐ **Schefflera**
- ☐ **Wandering Jew**

Special Plants

FOR KIDS

Imagine your children's delight when you help them plant some bulbs and they see them start to sprout and become pretty flowers. Or imagine how happy they will be when the cuttings they helped you make really develop roots and can be planted. They can start avocado or sweet potato plants on their own, too.

One word of caution — you may have to oversee the plant's care (let's not disappoint kids by letting their plants die). Describe the care plants need and help the kids take care of them properly. Show your children pictures of the following plants and let them select the ones they want to grow.

- ☐ **Coleus**
- ☐ **Grape Ivy**
- ☐ **Jade Plant**
- ☐ **Kalanchoe**
- ☐ **Peperomia**
- ☐ **Strawberry Begonia**
- ☐ **Swedish Ivy**
- ☐ **Wandering Jew**

NOT FOR KIDS

If you have children around the house who are still "rug rats" and love to put everything in their mouths, you may want to postpone getting some varieties of plants that are poisonous.

Consider that even plants that you could safely eat for breakfast may be growing in soil that's got lots of chemicals — insecticides, fertilizer, and so forth — in it. It's probably wise to treat every plant as though it were potentially dangerous to your children. And lock away your tools and supplies to prevent poisonings.

- ☐ **Aloe**
- ☐ **Arrowhead Plant**
- ☐ **Bittersweet**
- ☐ **Chrysanthemum**
- ☐ **Croton**
- ☐ **Daffodil and other bulb plants**
- ☐ **Dieffenbachia**
- ☐ **English Ivy**
- ☐ **Jerusalem Cherry**
- ☐ **Philodendron**
- ☐ **Poinsettia**
- ☐ **Pothos**
- ☐ **Schefflera**
- ☐ **Snake Plant**

Chapter 5

Tips for the Plant Owner

It seems that some people are able to care for their plants without the slightest effort. Others prune and prop, water and feed — and end up with brown, brittle sticks. The truth is, however, that there's no such thing as a green thumb. The folks who seem to slave and toil and still produce disasters just don't know the tricks and secrets of basic plant care.

This chapter is devoted totally to what to do and what not to do in caring for your plants. There are tips on watering, vacation care, moving with plants, along with many subjects you may not have thought of. When you read these tips, you'll think, "Right! That's the way to do it!" or "Gee, I hadn't thought of that." They'll make caring for your plants day in, day out, less work and more fun.

Watering

Coleridge wrote, "Water, water everywhere, but not a drop to drink." You would think he was lecturing on plant care, the way some people neglect watering their plants. Other people soak plants so often that they create muddy swimming pools. The best way to water plants is to follow the directions for each individual plant. Following are some tips to make the whole process a lot easier.

- Water the plant thoroughly so that the water runs out the bottom of the pot. That's what those drainage holes are for.

- Use lukewarm water. Ice cold water could give the plant a heart attack; water that's too hot could burn the roots.

- When the topsoil is just slightly moist, delay watering for one day. The soil below the surface will be moist enough to sustain the plant.

- Water in the morning rather than at night. This way, the plant has a chance to start using the water and won't fall asleep in a pool of it.

- To treat severe wilting, place the plant in a sink full of water for three hours. This will allow it to soak up all the water it wants or needs to start its revival. Repeat this process the next day. After that, return to your usual watering schedule.

- It's best not to water a plant in a plastic or ceramic pot as often as you would a plant in a clay pot. A plant in a ceramic pot will be able to go at least two days longer without water than one planted in a water-absorbent clay pot.

- Here's a tip for watering plants in pots with no drainage holes. Before planting anything in one, measure its capacity. Divide the capacity by four to find out how much water to pour in when you water. You can note that amount of water on tape and stick it in some inconspicuous spot on the pot if you have lots of plants to keep track of in nondraining containers. And remember that a pot with no drainage holes will not dry out as quickly as others that can drain, so don't water plants in one until the topsoil has been dry for a day.

- Use ice cubes to "water" hard-to-reach hanging plants without any drips at all.

Humidity

Stop and think for a minute about where most green plants originated. There are very few types that can't trace their family heritages back to some tropical forest. It's also true that there are fewer tropical forests that aren't humid. So it's logical to assume that green plants will need some extra humidity from time to time. (Growing plants can really be so simple — right?) Nevertheless, don't overdo it with that misting bottle of yours. Too much humidity can start to plague a plant with fungus.

There are a lot of little tricks to learn to get extra humidity up around a plant. Some of the best ways to do this are as follows.

- Fill a saucer with small rocks or gravel. Then fill the saucer with water. You can next place the pot with the plant on top of these rocks so the bottom is not sitting in the water. Nature does the rest. The water evaporates and keeps the air around the plant moistened. (This is an especially good idea to try in the winter when the humidity is low.)

- Clear plastic bags work wonders in emergency cases. The following idea could be called the recovery room trick. First, water your plant thoroughly. Then place it in a clear plastic bag. Before pulling the bag up around the plant, mist it and the inside of the bag to get extra moisture around the plant. Next, pull the bag up around the plant and secure it at the top with a twistem or string. Place the plant in a semi-sunny spot and leave it like this for twenty-four hours. Now the plant has its own little greenhouse. The whole idea is to get moisture to a plant when it needs it quickly.

- Large plants aren't hard to mist. You just need to think on a little larger scale. Put two or three in the shower and turn lukewarm water on gently. Let them enjoy the shower. They'll think they are back in their rain forest home. (This is also a good cure for the lack of humidity in the winter.)

Drainage

If you don't provide your plant with good drainage to start with, you might as well buy an artificial one and forget it. Poor drainage usually forces your plant to sit in water at one time or another. All kinds of hideous things will happen to make your ego and your plant's appearance go right down the drain — the pun intended. Poor drainage will rot the roots and soon there won't be enough root structure to support the plant. Your plant will start to wilt and so will your spirits. So it's important — and simple — to make sure your plants get the proper drainage. (See p. 72 for tips on watering plants that are potted in containers that lack drainage holes.)

- Use gravel or broken pottery as the bottom layer in pots when you repot plants, particularly if there are no drainage holes in the pot.
- Here's how to test for overwatering or poor drainage. Take the plant out of the pot and check the roots. If they are dark or blackish, they are rotting, the result of poor drainage. Roots that are healthy are always white or cream-colored.
- Take small plants to the kitchen sink to be watered. Allow the excess water to drain thoroughly from the drainage holes before returning them to their spot.
- What about that thin five- or six-foot schefflera in the living room, sitting in the pretty pot you bought at the auction last week? Place a layer of bricks across the bottom, one brick high. Put your plant on the bricks to lift it off the bottom of the decorative pot. This will allow you to water the plant, let the water drain out, and yet have space below the plant which will collect the extra water. Every two weeks, dump the excess water out, however, to be on the safe side and avoid any rotting.
- If dumping excess water out of such a large pot seems too hard to do, use a bulb-type meat baster to get it out.

Light

Light is one of those things a plant must have to stay alive. Without it, a plant cannot manufacture its food — it's that simple. Fortunately, there are plants that need different amounts of light (see the lists of bright- and low-light plants on p. 65 and the individual light requirements of plants in the "Plant Owner's Manual," pp. 89-102). But don't overdo the light show! Your poor plants need to rest just like you do. Ten to twelve hours is plenty for green plants. Up to sixteen hours will be adequate for flowering plants and cacti.

- It's no NEWS that there are north, east, west and south exposures. The varying intensities of light from them can make a difference in how plants will grow. *North:* ideal for some plants and artists. It's constant, shadowless, indirect light. *East:* good for those plants that like some good light, but not all day. East light, being morning light, isn't extremely hot. *West:* very bright light, usually quite hot. Be careful to protect plants against burning in west windows. *South:* again, very intense light, but it's constant too. Great for sun-loving plants, but do use caution here as well.

- Diffused light is slightly filtered, whether by a shade, a curtain, an overhang on the house, or trees outside. Diffused light can be bright, but isn't as hot as direct sunlight.

- Lamps are excellent sources of light, especially in the winter. Incandescent light can be one good source of auxiliary light. Don't put a plant too near a bulb, however, because its heat can scorch a plant's leaves. (How often have you burned your fingers trying to unscrew a bulb you've just turned off?) Fluorescent light is cooler than incandescent; the bulbs last longer too.

- Add a white reflector behind any incandescent or fluorescent bulb to get the maximum light available.

- A combination of incandescent and fluorescent light is good for plants and saves money. Keep a ratio of one watt of incandescent to five watts of fluorescent light if you combine sources.

- Light-colored walls reflect light; dark ones absorb it. Take this into consideration when placing your plants around the house. For example, a north-facing room painted white and filled with light-colored furniture will be lighter than an east-facing room that is panelled and filled with dark furniture.

- Always place a plant a bit away from the window glass. This is especially important with south or west exposures. The temperature just inside the glass can be extreme and will scorch the plant's leaves in the summer and stunt (or even freeze) them in the winter.

Temperature/Cleaning

Temperature

Temperatures can have drastic or rewarding effects on a plant. Proper temperatures make a plant thrive; drafts can make it wilt.

- A range of between 58° and 82°F. is perfect for most plants.

- Keep plants out of icy drafts in cold weather, and away from air conditioners when it's hot. Watch to see if the leaves move — if they do, the plant's in a draft. A drafty area can be 20° cooler than the rest of the room. The signal of danger? Wilting leaves.

- Don't put plants in front of or near heat sources, either. They'll start dropping leaves if they're overheated. But don't be alarmed if your plants drop a few leaves when the heat is first turned on. The plant will soon get used to the heat.

- A plant can easily tolerate a drop of ten degrees at night. Go ahead, turn down the thermostat. And for those plants nearest the window in the winter, pull the shade and drapes at night. Doing so will also help your fuel bills.

- Always allow enough air space between plants to let the air circulate around them. This will keep the temperature the same all around the plant.

Cleaning

It's very important to keep your plants' leaves clean — both tops and bottoms. The plant makes its food from the light it takes in on the top side of each leaf. And the underside is where it takes in the carbon dioxide it needs and gives off the oxygen we need.

- Once a month, put your plants in the kitchen sink and spray them with clear lukewarm water. This removes all the dust and grime from their surfaces. For larger plants, the shower is the place to do this (see page 73).

- Keeping your plants clean in this way also helps keep pests away. Bugs won't have a chance to take hold of a plant if it is kept sprayed and clean.

- Commercial plant shines are the best things to use to polish the leaves. They're made specifically for this purpose. Follow the directions and you'll have really pretty plants. Don't get any on the underside of the leaves, though. It will clog the pores that allow the plant to breathe.

- When hand polishing each leaf, put your hand under it for support. Otherwise the leaf could crack or tear as you work on it.

Tools

Growing these green friends of yours will be a lot easier if you have some tools to help you. It's just like any hobby or job: you need a few things to make it less work. I suggest that you keep all these tools together on a shelf in the closet or kitchen. That way you'll know where they are when you need them. Also, you won't get your tools mixed up with your kitchen utensils. Read on and see which of these you don't have (or do, but have used in different ways before).

- **An old fork.** Not for eating plants, of course, but for stirring up the soil. The roots love this, since it gets oxygen down to them.

- **Popsicle sticks.** On one side, put the name of the plant. On the other, put a little something about care. For example, "dry, bright" meaning, of course, dry soil, bright light. This way there's no excuse for overwatering them — and it's helpful for a friend who stops by to cover for you when you're out of town.

- **Lots of saucers.** They will be needed more than you know for catching drips, making natural humidifiers (see p. 73) — and serving snacks when they're scrubbed clean.

- **Measuring spoons** — sounds like we're cooking again. They should be used for measuring out fertilizer or insecticide. Don't get them mixed up with the ones you cook with.

- **Plastic pitcher.** Handy for mixing fertilizer or insecticide in. *Don't* use for lemonade.

- **A meat baster.** It is really handy in getting excess water out of pots that are too big or heavy to take to the kitchen sink.

- **Twistems or string.** Wonderful to have when you need to tie a plant to a stake. Don't twist too tight on the stem of the plant or you'll cut into it.

- **A good sharp scissors.** When you have to cut off a dead or diseased leaf, you'll want to give the stem a good clean cut. Make sure this tool is sharp — don't cut yourself.

- **Potting soil.** Once you open a bag of potting soil, close it up tightly after taking some out. If you don't the soil will dry and be very difficult to use.

Propagating

Propagating plants is fun and easy to do. Children delight in watching new plants form. Also, it's a good way to start new plants from an old one you want to discard because it's no longer attractive.

Don't be disappointed if all your new plants don't make it. They don't have 100% luck at green houses, either!

- Use equal parts of soil, sand and vermiculite for rooting cuttings. It's sufficiently light so new roots can develop and yet there is enough substance to hold the cuttings up.
- Always make sure that the parent plant is healthy. There's no sense in starting new diseased plants!
- *Stem cuttings.* Cuttings can be about three to six inches long. Use a sharp

knife and cut into the stem at an angle just below a leaf (Fig. 1a). Remove the bottom leaves of the cutting so you have a stem two to four inches long (Fig. 1b). Place this cutting along with others in a pot containing your moist potting material (Fig. 1c). Water this thoroughly and keep it out of direct sunlight for a few days. Keep the soil moist but not soggy wet in the days ahead. Mist foliage only occasionally (the plant cutting will take moisture in this way). Depending on the variety of plant, roots will start to appear in two to four weeks. A little tug on the cutting will let you know if roots have developed. If you get some resistance from this tug, they have started (Fig. 1d). Leave the plant for at least another week in the rooting material before taking it out and care-

Figure 1: Stem cutting

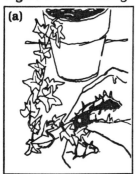   

Cut stem at angle.   *Strip off bottom leaves.*   *Place in moist soil*   *Roots grow in 2 to 4 weeks.*

Propagating

fully potting it in a potting mixture soil (see tips on repotting, p. 81). This technique works well with a wandering Jew, Swedish ivy, pothos, philodendron, impatiens, begonia or geranium.

- *Division.* Some plants develop in clumps, so they can easily be divided. Ferns, Chinese evergreen, and peace lily are just a few that can be divided this way. Simply remove the plant from its container. Take a sharp knife and cut down through the soil to separate these clumps. Pot individually to get new plants from old.

- *Air layering.* Air layering is much easier to do than it sounds. First, cut into the stem of the plant, one-third of the way through. Prop the cut open with a wooden match or toothpick (Fig. 2a. If the wound is not propped open, it will heal itself and no roots will appear.) Once you have inserted the prop, wrap the whole stem, wound and all, with wet sphagnum moss (Fig. 2b). Next, cover the entire sphagnum moss ball with plastic. Occasionally, open it and add a bit of water, reclosing the plastic tightly (Fig. 2c). In about six to eight weeks, this moss ball should be filled with roots. When enough roots are visible, cut this new plant away from the old one by cutting off the stem just below the moss ball (Fig. 2d). Remove the plastic wrapper and carefully plant the roots, moss and all, into a pot of soil. Dieffenbachia or rubber plants love to be air layered. How about that? A new plant.

- *Runners.* Many plants have runners that can easily be used to start new

Figure 2: Air layering

(a) *Prop cut open.*

(b) *Wrap with moss.*

(c) *Cover moss with plastic.*

(d) *Transplant in new pot.*

Propagating

plants. Strawberry begonias and spider plants are two good examples of this type of plant. Simply take the runners, still attached to the parent plant, and settle them into pots of soil surrounding the older plant. Secure the ends of the runners into the soil with v-shaped pieces of wire (hairpins work well). Before you know it, they will attach themselves into the soil by fine little roots. When these roots are well-developed, the new plant can be cut away from the older plant. It's not unusual to get ten or twelve new plants from an old strawberry begonia or spider plant this way.

- *Stem section.* This is a good way to start new dieffenbachia. Once they have grown tall and rangy, air layer the top to produce one new plant (see p. 79 for instructions). Cut off the remaining stem at about one inch above the soil line (Fig. 3a — more about what to do with the stump in a minute). Cut the stem you removed from the parent plant into sections, making sure there are two old leaf scars per section (Fig. 3b). Plant these *horizontally* just below the soil line in a pot of potting soil (Fig. 3c). Water regularly to keep the soil moist. Before you know it, roots will appear and the old pieces of stem will be sending up new leaves (Fig. 3d). Meanwhile, continue watering the stump of the parent plant, just as you always have. You've got a good chance of this old-timer sending up a new leaf and starting all over again. It's possible to get ten or twelve new plants this way, just from one old dieffenbachia.

Figure 3: Stem sectioning

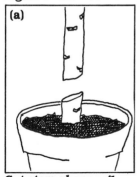

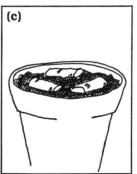

(a) Cut stem above soil line.

(b) Allow 2 leaf scars a section.

(c) Plant sections horizontally.

(d) Shoots start in 2 to 4 weeks.

Repotting

To repot or not to repot — that is the question. Wonder if that thought ever crossed Hamlet's mind. When it comes to repotting, there are a number of things to consider.

- Repot into a container that is only one inch or at most two inches larger in diameter than the existing pot.
- After you take the plant out of the old pot, place it quickly into its new home. It doesn't want to sit on the counter with its roots dangling too long.
- Do not break the root ball. This will disturb the roots too much and can really harm the plant.
- The best time to repot is in the middle of a plant's watering cycle. This way, the soil won't be too heavy with moisture or too dry and crumbly (either way, the root ball could fall apart). If it's inbetween — not too wet, not too dry — the soil will stick together and the root ball will stay intact.
- If a blooming plant needs to be repotted, wait until *after* it has finished blossoming.
- If you're using a container with a drainage hole, put a piece of broken crock over the hole so all the soil doesn't wash out. Then put one-half to one inch of finely broken crockery in the bottom of the pot. This just makes for better water drainage.
- After setting the root ball into the new pot, fill the gap between it and the pot with soil.
- Leave an inch between the top of the soil and the top of the pot. This will make it a lot easier to water. Pack the soil firmly, but not so tightly that the water cannot soak through.
- Soak the soil thoroughly after repotting. This will help reduce repotting trauma.
- If you're repotting into a clay pot, soak the pot in water for a few minutes before you repot. That way, it won't absorb the moisture out of the soil of its new tenant.

Topiary

Topiary art began in France, where shrubbery was trained to grow in unusual decorative shapes. Staking the plants and forcing them to grow to fit certain frames, along with constant pruning and shaping, creates shrubs and plants that look like animals or tiered balls. You can shape certain plants using topiary techniques and a little patience and thought. The tips that follow will help you achieve some unusual effects with your plants.

- Coleus, lantana, geraniums, hibiscus, weeping fig, and ligustrum are a few plants that can be grown easily into topiary shapes.
- Cut off all side branches of the plant. Leave the main stem intact (Fig. 4a).
- Place a stake in the soil and carefully attach the plant's main stem to the stake (Fig. 4b).
- Remove all new side shoots as they appear. This allows the main stem to grow taller.
- When your plant reaches the height you want, pinch out the center of growth in the main stem (Fig. 4c). This will force the branching out process that's now needed.
- Keep turning the plant so it gets even light and grows fuller.
- When it bushes out to the desired width, trim out all the shoots' center buds to make it get even thicker (Fig. 4d). You now have a ball-shaped plant to enjoy.
- If you're repotting into a clay pot, soak the pot in water for a few minutes before you repot. That way, it won't absorb the moisture out of the soil of its new tenant.

Figure 4: Topiary techniques

(a) *Trim off side growth.*

(b) *Stake plant.*

(c) *Pinch out center growth.*

(d) *Pinch or prune side growth.*

Espalier

Espalier is very much like topiary art. The main difference is that with espalier, the plant is trained to grow along a flat surface rather than being forced to grow in a fully rounded shape. Perhaps a trellis design on a wall or a candelabra pattern is the shape you might choose for an espalier treatment. To do it, follow these tips.

- Insert a wire frame shaped the way you want the plant to grow into the plant's pot very carefully (Fig. 5a).

- Attach the plant to the frame with twistems, filling in the empty spaces of the frame so it's as full of foliage as it can be at the moment (Fig. 5b).
- Keep pruning the ends so it will continue to branch out and fill in the frame (Fig. 5c).
- Again, keep turning the plant so it gets even light and grows evenly (Fig. 5d).
- Any of the ivies — grape ivy or English ivy, for example — and ligustrum are plants that are suitable for growing this way.

Figure 5: Espalier techniques

		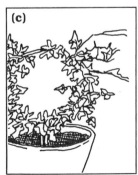	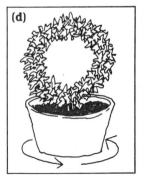
Insert wire frame.	*Attach plant to frame.*	*Prune to shape.*	*Turn regularly.*

Dish Gardening

There is nothing prettier than a mixture of plants all potted together to give variety of color and texture. A few helpful tips will make dish gardening easier and more successful.

- Don't overcrowd your plants. Often people plant the container so full, there's no place for the plants to grow. Sure, it looks pretty at first because it's compact and full-looking. Before long, however, a few leaves start to turn yellow and die due to the lack of space and light.
- Always select plants that like the same growing conditions. Peperomia and ivy look pretty side by side, but won't live together. They simply want different light and water conditions.

- Many decorative containers don't have any holes in the bottoms, so compensate for the lack of drainage (see pp. 72 and 74).
- Try a few interesting plants — anything will work, as long as it's in proportion to the container — planted in a low Chinese container. Plant them off-center; cover the soil with a light layer of sand and a few small rocks for a real Oriental garden effect.
- Here are some attractive combinations of plants that will peacefully co-exist; peperomia and dracaena godseffiana; English ivy and miniature ferns; pothos and philodendrons; wandering Jews and Swedish ivy (they almost look like a salad together!); cacti and succulents, for instance Jade trees; or begonias and impatiens.

Pests

Insects are all around us, and I have a hunch that they are not going to go away. Keeping your plants clean will help keep the insects off your plant in the first place, but if that preventive measure fails you, here are tips for coping with some typical pests.

- Aphids are tiny round sucking insects that seem to like the new growing tips of plants. They draw out all the plant's juices, causing curled, deformed leaves. Since aphids can be brought into the house on garden tools, wash them thoroughly before bringing them in. Clean garden plants with soap and water and give them a spray of insecticide before bringing them in, for the same reason. Use a systemic insecticide (applied to the soil) to rid your plants of aphids if you notice them or their damage.

- Earthworms can exist in unsterilized soil; they like to eat your plants' roots. A systemic insecticide will get rid of them, but if you use only sterilized soil, you shouldn't have to deal with them.

- Mealybugs look like little pieces of white cotton, and they'll usually be found along the leaf stem of plants. Like aphids, they are sucking insects. Curled or deformed leaves may be an indication that your plant has mealybugs. Use an insecticide to rid your plant of them. Spraying weekly for three or four weeks in a row should control them.

- Spider mites are microscopic pests, so the first sign of their presence is a light cobwebby effect on the leaf of a plant. The second sign of spider mites is leaf discoloration. To treat for them, spray the plant first with water to loosen the webs and get rid of some of the mites. Then use a spray insecticide. Repeat the water-and-insecticide treatment at two-week intervals until the mites disappear.

- Occasionally, microscopic insect eggs can be buried in a plant's soil or on its surfaces when you bring it home from the greenhouse. To determine if your new plant has brought you any unwelcome houseguests, check the plant closely to see if there are any signs of infestation about two or three weeks after you get it.

- Wash plants periodically with a mild solution of dishwashing (not dishwasher) detergent. Rinse them thoroughly after each washing. Note: this does not apply to fuzzy-leafed plants!

- Bear in mind that your hands can transfer pests as you move from plant to plant, so wash them well after treating infested ones.

- Always isolate infested plants and check other plants closely once you identify a problem. Insects may have jumped to neighboring plants' pots.

- If a plant is badly infested, it's best to give up and throw it away.

Cheapskate Tips

Most Plant for the Money

Plants are expensive. That's a fact of life. When purchasing a plant, therefore, you should look for and do a number of things to get the most for your money.

- Don't buy the first plant you see. Check it first for holes in the leaves, insects and just general appearance. Don't buy one with wilted, curled, deformed or yellowing leaves.
- Don't buy a plant just because you like it. Make sure it will grow in the light you will be giving it. Ask questions about its care before purchasing it.
- Watch for sales. Often florists and greenhouses have plant sales in the early spring and early fall. They need to make room for spring plants, and fall is the time poinsettias need so much care. You can get good buys at these times of year.
- If it's a floor plant you're looking for, don't buy a small version. It may take years for a small plant to become big enough to qualify for floor plant status.
- Whatever you do, *buy from a reputable plant dealer.* People at nurseries, greenhouses, and florists' shops are specialists in this field. You don't buy your car from the corner drugstore, so why buy your plants there?

Double-Duty Planters

Now that we've saved money on the plants, let's work on their pots.

- Egg cartons — great for seedlings and cuttings.
- Clay pots — classic good looks and good for your plant.
- Galvanized pails — good for large floor plants, but also cheaper and sturdier than large clay pots. Punch holes in the bottom.
- Wicker baskets — a great look to cover that galvanized pail. Use another for a wastebasket to create a coordinated look.
- Kitchen stuff — old teapots, sugar bowls, colorful mixing bowls and so on make nice additions to a kitchen when planted.
- Wire vegetable baskets — line with moss to hold soil and plant away! This idea is also fun with Grandma's old colander.
- Wooden crates — use a pyrex container as a liner.
- Mason jars — plants will grow well, plus you can watch root development. An old jug or aquarium will do the same trick.
- Lawn decorations — an old bird bath planted with grape ivy or a lovely Boston fern can do double duty for you too.

Cheapskate Tips

Free or Almost Free

Another way of getting the most for your money is to avoid spending it! If you do a few of the things listed below you'll have mastered the cheapskate approach. Really, when you think about it, *cheapskate* is just another word for practical.

- Trade cuttings. There are always people in the neighborhood who are looking for new cuttings. Give a cutting exchange coffee party in the spring, when plants are all set to start growing. (See p. 78 for propagating tips.)
- Start plants from seeds. You'll be amazed at how many varieties of seeds are available at your plant stores. This includes indoor green plant seeds as well as outdoor varieties.
- Don't forget avocado pits and sweet potatoes. They're easy to grow in water and will produce a lovely plant in not too much time. And really, what would you do with them anyway?
- Keep your geraniums wintered over in the house. They will become a little straggly, but if you take cuttings in March, you'll have nice new plants for the garden in May. Also, cut back the parent plant drastically after you take the cuttings you need. Give it lots of sunlight and you'll have a good stocky plant for the patio come spring.
- Recycle your Easter lilies in the garden. After the blossoms fade and the leaves start to yellow, plant the bulb in the garden in a sunny spot. The blooms you'll get in August will make you glad you didn't throw that plant away after the holiday.
- Poinsettias, kalanchoes, and mums are all seasonal blooming plants. They can all be grown year-round and brought back into bloom in the fall. Just remember they will only get their blossom if they have a short day. When that wonderful season called fall comes along, move them into a room that gets no more than the natural daylight. Soon you'll see buds on the mums and red leaves appear on the poinsettia. Not only does this save you money — but what a feeling of satisfaction!
- One of the best ways to save plant money is to invest a little in a supply of insecticides and fertilizers. When you spot a pest problem, you'll have the insecticide on hand to take care of this problem instead of letting the bugs keep chomping away while you try to remember to get the stuff.
- Don't repot a plant into a dirty pot (hot soapy water works wonders!). Otherwise, fungus can spread and zap! "There goes another rubber tree plant."
- Unless you make a tremendous amount and use it up quickly, buy your potting soil pre-mixed from a greenhouse. This will save you money and there's less waste in the long run.

Vacation Care/Moving

Vacation Care

So you decided to take the kids, Grandma, and Rover on a quick trip to the Grand Canyon. The tires have been checked, traveler's checks bought, picnic lunch packed. What about your green friends that you're leaving behind? They'll be all right, you say. You soaked them well before you left, and now the poor things are on their own. A few of the tricks listed below will help ensure that they'll be alive when you get home from the big trip.

- Water well before you leave.
- As extra insurance, put about two inches of water in the tub or kitchen sink. Set some bricks in the water so the tops are above water level. Next, place a plant on each brick. The water evaporating from the tub will help the plant survive until you return. (Do this only if the bathroom or kitchen is well-lighted. Poor light will kill the plants faster than dryness will.)
- Instead of all this, and particularly if you'll be gone a long while, break down and ask a neighbor to come in and water them. A little souvenir from the Grand Canyon will be cheaper than replacing some of your plants! Be sure to leave care instructions.

Moving

Your move will be easy if you do these things.

- For a short move across town, or for less than 24 hours in a truck, try this. Roll each plant up in paper. Make sure to place the leaves gently so their tips point towards the top of the plant. You can then pull the paper quite snuggly around the plant. Pack the wrapped-up plants fairly closely together in the moving truck so they won't tip and leaves won't get broken.
- If the move is a long one, try this instead. Wrap your plants in clear plastic, but leave the top open so air can get to the plant. Pack them in the truck last so they are closest to the door. When you make pit stops, open the doors so your plants get some light. This will keep them healthy for three or four days.
- Never put plants in the trunk of a car. In the winter, they will freeze; in the summer, they'll simply bake.
- If you need to move in cold weather, wrap newspaper around them first and then completely cover them with plastic. Close the plastic tightly so no freezing air can get to the plant.
- When you get to your new house, place the plants in the same exposures as in the old house. If it's not possible to do this, duplicate conditions as closely as possible.

Chapter 6

Plant Owner's Manual

Let's face the facts. Each variety of plant has its own water and light needs, plus its peculiar preferences and problems. Some are almost impossible to kill, no matter how badly you abuse or neglect them. Others seem downright temperamental, resisting your best efforts to make them happy and threatening your ego. But by and large most plants fall between those extremes.

In this chapter you'll see thumbnail sketches of the characters of the most popular plants. You may know them by other common names, but you'll recognize them by their portraits. For success with your friendly green plants, read the following pages. Treat plants right and you'll be amazed at what they'll do for you. (They won't do windows!)

Arrowhead Plant
Syngonium podophyllum or Nephthytis

RATING

Ah, so easy. A vining type plant that will look lovely dripping from a shelf in a bookcase, or cascading over the edge of a table.

WATER

Moist soil is the rule. Dry soil makes a more compact plant.

LIGHT

Anywhere, anywhere, anywhere. Isn't that wonderful to hear?

TIPS

Allow these plants to get enough water and they will grow their fool heads off. They can also be trained to grow up a pole.

PROBLEMS

None to speak of. A leaf or two may turn yellow occasionally, but that's natural. The leaves just get old and want to quit.

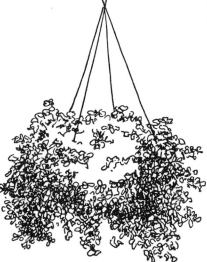

Baby Tears *Helxine soleirolii*

RATING

Easy to grow and well worth the effort.

WATER

This plant never, never wants to be dry. Evenly moist soil will help it spread into a lovely mound of greenery.

LIGHT

Baby tears do beautifully in an east or north window. Never, never put them in a south window or you're asking for trouble.

TIPS

Don't panic when they start to shed all their leaves. Baby tears do this annually and soon start sending out new leaves to replace all the lost ones. For a tiered cascade effect, plant a six-inch clay pot full of baby tears. Set it on top of the soil of an eight-inch pot. Then fill the outer edge of the eight-inch pot with more baby tears.

PROBLEMS

No real problems; just don't forget the water.

Boston Fern
Nephrolepsis exaltata bostoniensis. What a handle!

RATING
Moderately easy to grow.

WATER
It's essential to a fern's existence that it be kept evenly moist. Never allow one to dry out — or to sit in water. Mist *occasionally.*

LIGHT
It will do best in bright diffused light.

TIPS
Boston ferns will grow into stately beauties in no time if you mist them occasionally and keep them root-bound.

PROBLEMS
The center of a fern has a tendency to die out. If this happens, simply cut away the dead fronds so new ones can take their place. Shake the plant really hard once a week to rid it of all dead or dying leaves ... before you vacuum.

Chinese Evergreen *Aglaonema modestum*

RATING
Excellent! This plant will grow where no other one will.

WATER
A Chinese evergreen is one of those plants that likes it a little on the dry side between soakings. Always make sure it is watered so that the water drains out the bottom. This ensures that the whole root ball is well-saturated.

LIGHT
Believe it or not, anywhere!

TIPS
These are truly beginners' plants. Their broad leaves lend them a sturdy, stately effect and won't give you any problem at all. "Advanced" plant people enjoy them, too. So, go ahead and invest in one or two of these beauties. You won't be sorry.

PROBLEMS
Absolutely none! I repeat, none! Isn't that music to your ears? A plant that won't give any problems is a plant to love and enjoy.

Coleus *Trailing Nettle; Painted Nettle*

RATING

Easy to grow and easy to propagate from stem cuttings.

WATER

Coleus like to be kept evenly moist to avoid leaf-wilting. Moist soil also keeps coleus blossoms fresh much longer.

LIGHT

The brighter the light, the brighter the foliage. That's the wonderful fun of coleus plants. They come in such marvelous jewel shades!

TIPS

Some varieties cascade beautifully. These, grown in hanging baskets, will make any patio or porch a very colorful summer place. Lush pots of coleus plants really look super set into (not planted in) copper or brass containers.

PROBLEMS

Coleus can attract mealybugs (see p. 85).

Corn Plant
Dracaena fragrans massangeana

RATING

Growing a corn plant is as easy as eating corn on the cob.

WATER

If you're prone to watering your plants whenever you think about it, rather than on a schedule, this one is for you. Overwatering will make the leaves turn yellow; however, moderate watering will make this plant flourish.

LIGHT

How about this? It will grow in full sun or shade.

TIPS

If your plant gets too tall for your taste, simply cut it off. Before you know it, you'll have another one (see p. 78). Corn plants also develop a beautiful flower that looks much like a lilac. And it's just as fragrant.

PROBLEMS

Virtually problem-free. Just keep their leaves clean.

Croton *Codiaeum*

RATING
Crotons are delightful plants to have in your collection. Their variety of color makes them an added attraction to any room. They are so easy to grow, if only given enough sunlight. That's the trick.

WATER
The soil should never be allowed to dry out, but on the other hand, they won't tolerate constantly soggy soil. Evenly moist soil is the key.

LIGHT
The brighter the light, the better. Crotons will grow in a shady area, but only sunlight will develop the bright, happy colors true to the croton plant.

TIPS
Because of their brilliant colors, they look especially pretty in the brightly-colored pottery or plastic pots that are so popular now. Try a shiny brass container for a dressier effect.

PROBLEMS
The only problem is in the watering: do it frequently.

Dieffenbachia *Dieffenbachia*

RATING
Easy as one-two-three to grow.

WATER
This is one of those wonderful plants that likes to have its soil dry out between thorough waterings. Great for dual-career households.

LIGHT
Another plant that loves two or three hours of sunlight each day.

TIPS
Dieffenbachia will grow into big, beautiful floor plants when given the chance. Often their stems will become twisted, which adds a truly dramatic effect to the looks of the plant. Different varieties produce different-sized leaves. Make sure that you ask about what variety you're buying (See p. 78.)

PROBLEMS
Dieffenbachia are not poisonous, but don't eat a leaf. Seriously, if part of a leaf is swallowed, it can paralyze a person's vocal chords for one or two hours.

Plant Owner's Manual

Dracaena Marginata
Dracaena marginata — alias Dragon Tree

RATING

Easy, easy, easy!

WATER

Porous soil and good drainage will help your watering of this plant. Don't water every day because it will tolerate drier soil.

LIGHT

Will do well in the shade but will also grow in strong light.

TIPS

As new leaves develop, the plant will discard some of the lower, older leaves. Don't be alarmed; that's just the pattern with dragon trees. Less is more — that's the philosophy here. As it gets older, it also will grow into interesting, artsy shapes with stems forming strange, wonderful angles and twists.

PROBLEMS

None. They're trouble-free, so buy one — they're great!

False Aralias
Dizygotheca elegantissima, Polyscias balfouriana

RATING

Somewhat difficult, but believe me, they're worth it.

WATER

This plant has a great big secret: it will drop a lot of dried-up leaves if it isn't kept moist. But don't overdo the watering. Stay sensible!

LIGHT

Aralias will do best if they can see at least two or three hours of sunlight each day, but they don't need much more. On an extremely hot, sunny day, pull a sheer drape or a shade just to diffuse the light a little.

TIPS

Just watch the light and water treatment.

PROBLEMS

Aralias *will* drop leaves as they grow larger, and the new ones get quite big. They often take on tree-like proportions as they grow.

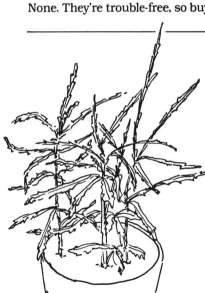

Grape Ivy *Cissus rhombifolia*

RATING

Easy, no problem, beginner's luck, simple.

WATER

Soak well and allow them to get a bit dry before rewatering.

LIGHT

They will do best in bright light, but will live in lower light atmospheres.

TIPS

Keep them clean. Red spider mites and mealybugs often like grape ivies as friends and meals. If properly cared for, grape ivies will grow into large, trailing beauties. It's not unusual for them to grow up a brick wall. They are worth your attention.

PROBLEMS

The only problem will be those pests I mentioned above. Keep plants well-cleaned and the problem disappears.

Jade Plant *Crassula argentea*

RATING

Simple to grow.

WATER

The biggest foe of this plant is water. Allow your jade to dry out and remain dry for a number of days before soaking it again. Because it's a succulent, it retains water in its leaves. Therefore, if you overdo the water, it will rot the plant.

LIGHT

Full sun. The more, the merrier. This plant will thrive and eventually blossom if given full brilliant sun (but avoid midday sun). The blossoms usually appear in December or January.

TIPS

Jades can be kept in relatively small pots for the size of the plant. Their root structure is quite small. Also, use a sand and soil potting mixture for best results.

PROBLEMS

Few and far between.

Norfolk Island Pine *Araucaria heterophylla*

RATING

Easy to grow as long as it is given the care below.

WATER

Water thoroughly. *Never* let it sit in water.

LIGHT

Direct sunlight isn't good for Norfolk pines. East or north windows are fine. A filtered west window is the next alternative.

TIPS

These regal plants grow to two hundred feet in their natural environment. Fortunately, you really don't have to worry about this happening in your home. You don't have the right conditions, the right sized pot for such a giant, or even the slightest chance of living long enough to see it happen. Keeping your Norfolk Island pine root-bound will keep it from getting too large.

PROBLEMS

Problems really don't exist for these plants. The only thing they don't like is a draft — cold or hot.

Palms *Palmae* — Areca, Kentia, and others

RATING

Easy to grow — no hidden tricks here.

WATER

When watering, allow the water to soak all the way through the pot and drain out. Keep the soil moist but don't ever let a palm sit in water.

LIGHT

Your palm loves it when it's in the light. Occasionally it will tolerate a lack of sunlight, but not for long.

TIPS

A palm is one of those wonderful plants that have a great relaxing effect on mere humans. Use one or two to create an oasis in your busy life.

PROBLEMS

The tips of a palm's fronds can sometimes turn brown from the effects of bruising cold drafts or from the hot sun. A simple diagonal cut with the scissors will take care of the problem.

Peace Lily (or Spathe Plant)
Spathiphyllum horibundum

RATING

There couldn't be an easier or prettier plant to grow.

WATER

Likes very much to be on the moist side. A signal of overwatering is yellow tips. Water thoroughly every five or six days.

LIGHT

Good light but not direct sunlight. These beauties will grow in even a shady spot.

TIPS

One of the enchanting things about this plant is its blossom, which is very pretty, is shaped almost like a Calla lily, and is highly scented. Of course, the more light, the more it will blossom. It is an extremely dense plant. To propagate, divide the roots (see p. 79).

PROBLEMS

There is only one problem I see with this plant. It is so pretty and easy to grow, you may cultivate too many of them.

Peperomia
Peperomia — alias Crinkle Leaf; Watermelon Plant

RATING

Easy to grow. This plant only grows about six inches high and stays nice and chunky, so have a number of them in your house.

WATER

Peperomias love to be allowed to get dry between waterings. Never allow them to stand in water.

LIGHT

They thrive in full sunlight. If placed in a darker part of a room, they have a tendency to get leggy.

TIPS

These plants come in a variety of colors. They grow only about six inches high so they look especially nice on a low shelf or desk.

PROBLEMS

Peperomias are really problem-free. Bugs and pests don't like them, so there's no problem there. Just don't overwater.

Pothos (or Devil's Ivy)
Scindapsus aureus

RATING
Grow these all over the house. They are so easy to grow, you won't even realize they are around.

WATER
Keep them on the dry side. Every month, mix some fertilizer in the water and water the plant with this solution. They don't need misting.

LIGHT
The only light they don't like is really hot summer sun.

TIPS
Pothos will grow in cascades from hanging baskets, and they can also be trained to grow up a pole as floor plants.

PROBLEMS
No problems — just enjoyment.

Prayer Plant *Maranta*

RATING
Simple, but mist it if the air is dry.

WATER
Soil must be kept moist at all times. Misting two or three times a week will make this beauty thrive.

LIGHT
Direct sunlight is a no-no. Try a north or east window for an ideal growing situation. A bathroom or kitchen is an ideal place to grow these treasures because of the extra moisture usually found in these areas.

TIPS
A prayer plant could be an enjoyable plant in a child's room. It's nicknamed *prayer plant* because its leaves close up at night as if it were praying.

PROBLEMS
None.

Rubber Plant *Ficus elastica*

RATING

Easy, easy, easy. And that's the truth.

WATER

Regular watering, yes, but not misting.

LIGHT

The brighter the better, your rubber plant will say. It will grow and grow, if put in a good west or south exposure.

TIPS

Rubber plants can easily be propagated by air layering (see p. 79). The rubber plant will also branch out where you make your cut and become a many-branched beauty. Another tip: support a leaf with your hand and polish it with a soft cloth — the natural wax will gleam.

PROBLEMS

For years we thought the good old rubber plant would grow any-where, under any conditions. It's tough, but not that tough.

Schefflera
Brassaia actinophylla — alias Umbrella Plant

RATING

So easy to grow you'll want lots of these beauties.

WATER

Let the soil get just a little dry between waterings before soaking it thoroughly.

LIGHT

A schefflera loves to sunbathe at least three hours a day. It will live in a north-facing room, but the growth rate will become almost nil.

TIPS

Scheffleras will grow to sixty feet or more, if properly taken care of. Feel free to cut it back drastically. You'll be pleasantly surprised at how fast it will branch out and start all over again.

PROBLEMS

Watch for red spider mites (see p. 85).

Plant Owner's Manual

Snake Plant *Sansevieria trifasciata*

RATING
They're called mother-in-law's tongue and maybe that's because you can't get rid of them. Sorry about that — I'm just joking.

WATER
Let the soil get thoroughly dry before you soak them.

LIGHT
The wonderful thing about these plants is that they will grow anywhere. I've often been tempted to leave one in the closet for a few weeks to see what would happen.

TIPS
Grow these beauties in full sun and watch them bloom. A fragrant white blossom will appear once a year. They will look stunning in an Art Deco room, or in any very contemporary, sleekly decorated room.

PROBLEMS
None. Absolutely none. Isn't that a relief? The only problem I can see is that all mothers-in-law will hate me.

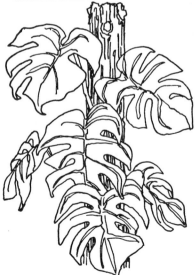

Splitleaf Philodendron
Monstera deliciosa — delicious monster?

RATING
Simple. Easy. A nothing-to-it plant.

WATER
A splitleaf will tolerate your neglect. If you're the type that forgets to water plants, have lots of philodendrons around.

LIGHT
Will grow anywhere — full sun, no sun, a little sun — you name it.

TIPS
As a philodendron grows older it has a tendency to stop growing those pretty split leaves. Good watering, misting and full sun will help to encourage your philodendron to keep on splitting. The lovely brown air roots that grow from the main stems of the plant can be trimmed off if you prefer. They're just to help the plant cling to the trees in the jungle and to give Tarzan something to swing on.

PROBLEMS
None.

Sprengeri Fern
Asparagus densiflorus 'Sprengeri'

RATING

Much easier to grow than a true fern.

WATER

Soak it thoroughly; allow it to drain well and get a bit dry before watering again. I don't mean like the Sahara Desert. If you do, you'll find all the little needles on the floor.

LIGHT

Good old filtered sunlight is the key to success. They can easily be grown indoors or out, year after year.

TIPS

A few pieces of their fern-like foliage can be so pretty when added to a fresh flower bouquet. Old ones can sometimes become a little sparse looking. I prefer to think of them as "arty" looking. These can really add drama to a contemporary room.

PROBLEMS

Just remember enough light and water.

Swedish Ivy *Plectranthus australis*

RATING

Not as stubborn as Swedes are supposed to be; however, this plant *will* just keep growing.

WATER

Keep moist, but not soggy wet. The soil should not be allowed to become dry for too long a period in between waterings. Make sure it's well-drained. Mist only occasionally, if your home is very dry.

LIGHT

Swedish ivy plants will tolerate many light conditions. Bright, hot, intense sunlight has a tendency to burn them. Diffused west or south light is good, or just a natural east exposure will do. North light will make them get a little stringy.

TIPS

Occasionally they will have to be cut back. You do this to make them branch out and fill in.

PROBLEMS

None, whatsoever!

Wandering Jew *Tradescantia fluminensis*

RATING

Buy these for no-care plants.

WATER

Water them freely, but don't let them sit in water.

LIGHT

Will thrive like everything in diffused light, but stronger light brings out their colors.

TIPS

Easy to propagate from stem cuttings. Also, trim back occasionally to make these colorful plants branch out and get thicker.

PROBLEMS

The only problem could be that a wandering Jew can get a little stringy-looking with age. Cut it back periodically, every six or seven months, to keep it bushy.

Weeping Fig *Ficus benjamina*

RATING

Moderately difficult to grow — but they're worth the trouble.

WATER

Water this plant thoroughly each week; never allow the soil to dry out.

LIGHT

A weeping fig loves three or so hours of direct sunlight each day. However, it will grow slowly in a north-facing window as long as the room itself is light and airy.

TIPS

Weeping figs like to get used to one spot and stay there. Move the loveseat, but not the Ficus. Let it sit in a tray of water for two or three hours after watering, so it can soak up all the water it needs.

PROBLEMS

Weeping figs always drop some leaves when first in a new home, but the problem should clear up in about two weeks, once the plant is used to its new home.

Index

FREE STUFF BOOKS

FREE STUFF FOR KIDS
Over 250 of the best free and up-to-a-dollar things kids can get by mail:
- coins & stamps
- bumper stickers & decals
- posters & maps

$3.45 ppd.

FREE STUFF FOR COOKS
Over 250 of the best free and up-to-a-dollar booklets and samples cooks can get by mail:
- cookbooks & recipe cards
- money-saving shopping guides
- seeds & spices

$3.45 ppd.

FREE STUFF FOR PARENTS
Over 250 of the best free and up-to-a-dollar booklets and samples parents can get by mail:
- sample teethers
- booklets on pregnancy & childbirth
- sample newsletters

$3.45 ppd.

FREE STUFF FOR HOME & GARDEN
Over 350 of the best free and up-to-a-dollar booklets and samples homeowners and gardeners can get by mail:
- booklets on home improvement & energy
- plans for do-it-yourself projects
- sample seeds

$3.45 ppd.

FREE STUFF FOR TRAVELERS
Over 1000 of the best free and up-to-a-dollar publications and products travelers can get by mail:
- guidebooks to cities, states & foreign countries
- pamphlets on attractions, festivals & parks
- posters, calendars & maps

$3.45 ppd.

Craig Olson's DECORATING WITH PLANTS
Creative, simple ideas for decorating with plants and caring for them—from the most entertaining plant expert in America. Illustrated and indexed.

$3.45 ppd.

Books By Vicki Lansky

Hundreds of parent-tested ideas for the first five years. Includes topics such as baby care, feeding, self esteem and more. **Spiral bound. $4.45 ppd.**

The most popular baby book and tot food cookbook for new parents. Includes over 200 recipes and ideas. **Spiral bound. $4.45 ppd.**

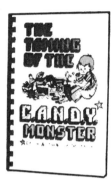

The classic cookbook that helps you get your children to eat less sugary, salty junk food . . . and like it! **Spiral bound. $4.45 ppd.**

The most complete, up-to-date, helpful, entertaining and gifty baby name book ever. Includes over 10,000 names. Introduction by Erma Bombeck. **$3.45 ppd.**